THE PEOPLE OF
CAMBODIA

Dolly Brittan

The Rosen Publishing Group's
PowerKids Press™
New York

Published in 1997 by The Rosen Publishing Group, Inc.
29 East 21st Street, New York, NY 10010

First Edition

Book Design: Danielle Primiceri

Photo Credits: Cover (background) © John W. Banagan/Image Bank, © Tom and Michele Grimm/ International Stock; pp. 4, 11, 16 © Josef Beck/FPG International; pp. 7, 12, 19 (all images) © Joe Viesti/Viesti Associates; pp. 8, 15, 20 © Dennie Cody/FPG International.

Brittan, Dolly.
   The people of Cambodia / Dolly Brittan.
      p. cm. (Celebrating the peoples and civilizations of Southeast Asia)
   ISBN 0-8239-5129-4
   1. Cambodia—Juvenile literature. I. Title. II. Series.
   DS554.3.B75 1997
   959.6—dc21   97-7982
    iB   CIP
                                                                 AC

Manufactured in the United States of America

Contents

The Country of Cambodia   5

A Hard History   6

The Land   9

The People   10

The Language   13

Religion   14

Angkor Wat   17

Festivals   18

The Food   21

Cambodia Today   22

Glossary   23

Index   24

VIETNAM

LAOS

THAILAND

South China
Sea

CAMBODIA

Phnom Penh

Gulf of
Thailand

The Country of Cambodia

Cambodia (kam-BOH-dee-uh) is a country in Southeast Asia. Its full name is the Kingdom of Cambodia. Cambodia is surrounded by the countries of Laos, Vietnam, and Thailand. To the south is the Gulf of Thailand. The capital of Cambodia is **Phnom Penh** (PNOM PEN). Phnom Penh is also the largest city.

Cambodia's history goes back to the first century. It has had many rulers. Cambodia was protected from its enemies by France from 1863 until 1953. After that, Cambodia was **independent** (in-dee-PEN-dent) once again.

Cambodia is a mix of the old and the new. This young girl is standing in the doorway of a building that was built hundreds of years ago.

A Hard History

In 1975, a group called the **Khmer Rouge** (KMER ROOZH), led by a man named Pol Pot, took over the country. Pol Pot wanted to rule the country his way. He hated and tormented everyone who didn't believe what he believed. He killed nearly 2 million people. In 1978, Vietnam helped Cambodia fight the Khmer Rouge. The fighting finally ended in 1991. It was agreed that Cambodia would not be run by Pol Pot, but by a king with the help of a **democratic** (dem-uh-KRAT-ik) government.

The king of Cambodia lives in the Royal Palace in Phnom Penh. ▶

The Land

The land in Cambodia is very **fertile** (FER-tul). It is good for growing crops, such as rice and rubber trees. About half of Cambodia is covered with **tropical** (TROP-ih-kul) forests. The forests are filled with many different trees. The wood from some trees, such as the teakwood and rosewood trees, are used to make things like ships and furniture.

The largest river in Cambodia is the Mekong River. The largest lake is Tonle Sap, which means "Great Lake." Cambodia is sunny much of the year.

◀ *Much of Cambodia is green with forests and fields.*

The People

Nearly 11 million people live in Cambodia. Most of the people in Cambodia are **Khmer** (KMER). Many Khmers are farmers. Many of these farmers live in small villages. There, people raise crops such as rice and vegetables. Some people weave their own cloth and make some of the things they use every day, such as pots, pans, and dishes. Most **rural** (RUR-ul) houses are built on stilts. Stilts keep the houses above the floods that often happen during the heavy rains that fall from May to October. Some people live in cities. Many of these people are doctors, lawyers, or teachers.

Many farmers bring their goods to the local market to sell. ▶

The Language

Most people in Cambodia speak the language Khmer. Khmer is similar in many ways to Lao, the language spoken in Laos, and Thai, the language spoken in Thailand. Like Lao and Thai, Khmer is a **tonal** (TOH-nul) language. That means that the same word can mean different things if you change the sound of your voice when you say the word.

Some older Khmers also speak and read French. Many younger Khmers speak, read, and write English.

Most people in Cambodia, including these Khmer dancers, speak the language Khmer.

13

Religion

Most Khmers practice a religion called **Buddhism** (BOOD-izm). Buddhists follow the teachings of a man called the Buddha. Buddha means "**enlightened** (en-LY-tend) one." Enlightenment is the complete understanding of life and of your place in life. Buddhism affects many parts of the Khmer's daily life.

There are many statues of Buddha throughout Cambodia. Some are huge. Others are tiny enough to fit in your hand. Every Khmer boy is expected to be a Buddhist **monk** (MUNK) for at least a few years.

Young Buddhist monks live, study, and learn with other monks. ▶

Angkor Wat

There are many Buddhist **temples** (TEM-pulz) in Cambodia. The Cambodian word for temple is *wat*. Many temples were built during the Angkor period of Cambodian history. This period was from the 800s to the 1400s. The most famous temple is Angkor Wat. It was built during the 1200s. It is one of the largest and most beautiful temples in the world. Much of Angkor Wat has become overgrown with many plants and trees. Many people visit Angkor Wat. Some people, such as monks, still pray there.

◀ *People from all over the world visit Angkor Wat.*

Festivals

The Khmers celebrate different festivals throughout the year. The biggest is Bon Om Tuk, or the Water Festival. It begins in late October or early November, around the end of the rainy season. **Pirogue** (pih-ROHG) races are held on the rivers. Pirogues are long, narrow boats. The boats are decorated with bright lights for the races. After the races, everyone gathers to watch fireworks.

In April, the Khmers celebrate Chaul Chnam. This is the celebration of the Khmer New Year. It lasts for three days.

There are many parts to the celebration of Chaul Chnam. Musicians, dancers, and even the king all take part in the ▶ celebration.

The Food

Rice is the main food of the people of Cambodia. Rice is often eaten with vegetables and sometimes fish or meat. Some dishes are flavored with spicy chili peppers. A favorite dish is grilled fish wrapped in lettuce or spinach. This is dipped into a nutty fish sauce. Many meals are served with a bowl of soup. Slices of fresh fruit, such as papaya, pine-apple, or mango, are eaten too. Some people drink coconut milk, the liquid found inside a coconut. Others drink soda water flavored with lemon.

There are many kinds of food in Cambodia. These women are selling food at a market.

Cambodia Today

The Kingdom of Cambodia has a long and interesting history. Visitors can see examples of the Khmer **culture** (KUL-cher) throughout Cambodia. There are more than 100 temples and many statues of the Buddha. The National Museum was once the home of the king of Cambodia. Today, it also houses beautiful Khmer crafts. The people of Cambodia have lived through many hard times. But the people and their culture have survived for nearly 1,000 years. Today, people around the world are taking an interest in this country. It is an exciting time for the people of Cambodia.

Glossary

Buddhism (BOOD-izm) A religion based on the teachings of the Buddha.

Cambodia (kam-BOH-dee-uh) A country in Southeast Asia.

culture (KUL-cher) The beliefs, customs, and art of a group of people.

democratic (dem-uh-KRAT-ik) A type of government run by the people.

enlightened (en-LY-tend) Having an understanding of yourself and the world that you live in.

fertile (FER-tul) Able to produce many crops.

independent (in-dee-PEN-dent) To think and act for yourself.

Khmer (KMER) A group of people in Cambodia. It is also the name of the language spoken by most people in Cambodia.

Khmer Rouge (KMER ROOZH) A political group in Cambodia.

monk (MUNK) A man who studies a religion.

Phnom Penh (PNOM PEN) The capital of and largest city in Cambodia.

pirogue (pih-ROHG) A long, narrow boat.

rural (RUR-ul) Having to do with the country instead of the city.

temple (TEM-pul) A place of worship.

tonal (TOH-nul) Having to do with the tone, or sound, of something.

tropical (TROP-ih-kul) Very hot and humid.

Index

A
Angkor Wat, 17

B
Buddha, the, 14, 22
Buddhism, 14
  enlightenment, 14

C
cities, 10
crops, 9, 10
culture, 22

F
farmers, 10
festivals
  Bon Om Tuk (Water
    Festival), 18
  Chaul Chnam (Khmer
    New Year), 18

food, 21
forests, tropical, 9

D
government,
    democratic, 6

I
independence, 5

K
Khmer, 10, 13, 14,
    18, 22
Khmer Rouge, 6
king, 6

L
language, 13

M
Mekong River, 9
monk, 14, 17

P
Phnom Penh, 5
pirogue, 18
Pot, Pol, 6

R
religion, 14

T
temples, 17, 22
Tonle Sap (Great
    Lake), 9

V
villages, 10

24